THE TABLETOP LEARNING SERIES

PAPER CAPERS

With Paper, Scissors, Glue and You
by Imogene Forte

Incentive Publications, Inc.
Nashville, Tennessee

Illustrated by Marta Zellars
Cover designed by Mary Hamilton and illustrated by Becky Cutler
Edited by Susan Oglander

Library of Congress Catalog Number 84-62932
ISBN 0-86530-097-6

THE TABLETOP LEARNING SERIES™ is a trademark of Incentive Publications, Inc., Nashville, TN 37215

THIS
PAPER CAPERS BOOK
BELONGS TO

_____

CONTENTS

ix   Be a Paper Saver

THINGS TO DO WITH PAPER AND GLUE

12   Fancy Fans
14   Stencil Magic
15   Crazy Quilt Place Mats
16   Star Light, Star Bright
17   Paint with Paper
18   Weave It and Leave It
20   All Beaded Up
21   Foiled Again
22   Birds of a Feather Fly Together
23   Doorknob Decorations
24   The Chain Gang
25   Mark the Place with a Smiling Face
26   Mural, Mural on the Wall
28   Birthday Book Bonanza
30   Greetings Designed To Please
33   A Many-Colored Creature and His Twin
36   Easy Envelopes
38   Fun and Fancy Hats
40   Kaleidoscope Designs
42   Frame-Ups

STAND BY FOR STAND-UPS

46   On a Roll
47   Cut-Ups
48   Tell the Story
50   Magic Lanterns
52   Circle Go Round
53   The Tree Stands Alone
54   Ring-A-Rounds
56   Cardboard Is Not Boring
57   Tissue Paper Flowers
58   Peep and Tell
60   Two by Two
62   Bug-A-Boo
63   Paper Building Pieces
66   A Zig Here, a Zag There
67   Arms and Legs — Collars and Frills

SPRUCE UP SOME OLD STANDARDS

70   Sailing, Sailing
71   Not-So-Newsy Notes
72   Ways To Use Paper Bags
74   Ways To Use Paper Plates
76   Ways To Use Paper Cups
78   INDEX

BE A PAPER SAVER

As you begin to discover some of the wonderful things you can do with paper, you will want to save every scrap of paper you find. Many of the projects in **Paper Capers** can be made from paper which has already been used. Be on the lookout for scraps of special papers to recycle and add interest to your paper creations, too. Many of your finds will need to be pressed with a warm iron to erase creases and wrinkles. Others will need to be trimmed to get rid of frayed or torn edges. Some should be rolled while others may be stored flat. A big, flat box such as the kind suits or coats come in makes a good storage container. To complete your paper collection add glue, scissors and various odds and ends such as felt, fabric scraps, string and ribbon. Start your paper collection with some of the following, then find more sources of your own.

- gift wrap
- brown wrapping paper
- tissue paper
- cellophane
- foil
- paper doilies
- newspaper
- interesting pages from magazines
- junk mail
- envelopes
- corrugated paper
- greeting cards
- travel brochures
- catalogs
- wallpaper
- empty cereal boxes, can labels
- old calendars
- scraps of construction paper

Many print shops have paper scraps that they have no use for, and some wallpaper stores give away their outdated sample books. You just might be lucky enough to be there at the right time to ask for these "leftovers." Ask your friends and relatives for contributions, too. Before you know it, you'll have a box full of goodies and be all set for "paper capers" of any sort.

Imogene Forte

THINGS TO DO WITH PAPER AND GLUE

FANCY FANS

It is said that grand ladies in olden times would never have gone out without their elegant fold-up paper fans. They used these fans to cover their faces, to stir up a breeze when the air was stale and even to keep unwanted insects away. But most of all, the purpose of a beautiful fold-up fan was the sense of pride and pleasure it gave to its owner. The fancier the fan, the prouder the "fanner."

WHAT TO USE:
- large sheet of paper
- scissors
- string or ribbon

WHAT TO DO:
1. Cut a long strip of paper.
2. Make a fold at one end of the strip.
3. Reverse the strip and fold it again.
4. Fold forward, then backward until you have pleated the entire strip.
5. Tie the strip with a ribbon or string and unfold it carefully.

Make a plain fan or two for practice, and then you will be ready to try your hand at some fancy fan making.

Try cutting stars, circles, hearts, triangles, squares or other objects on the pleated fold. Open it up to see the beautiful designs you have made.

Then try slits and other cutouts of your own making. You can use this same kind of paper folding to make angel wings, collars, cuffs, ruffles and holiday decorations.

STENCIL MAGIC

WHAT TO USE:
- heavy cardboard
- scissors
- paper
- paint or felt tip pens

WHAT TO DO:
1. Cut out a favorite shape or the letters of your name.
2. You can then use either the positive or negative of the stencil for decorative note cards, stationery or for "made-by-you" wrapping paper.
3. Place your stencil on a piece of paper. Paint or color the inside or outside of the stencil. Keep all the stencils you make in a convenient place to use again and again.

CRAZY QUILT PLACE MATS

WHAT TO USE:
- scraps of paper (fancy gift wrap, envelope linings, etc.)
- construction paper
- felt tip pens
- glue

WHAT TO DO:
1. Arrange the paper scraps on the construction paper to recreate an old-fashioned random-piece pattern.
2. Glue the scraps in place.
3. Use the felt tip pens to add decorative trim comparable to the fancy stitches needleworkers used.

Celebrate your work by using the place mats for a special family meal!

STAR LIGHT, STAR BRIGHT

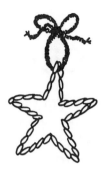

WHAT TO USE:
- construction paper
- pencil
- waxed paper
- yarn
- glue
- glitter (if you have it)

WHAT TO DO:
1. Draw a star on a sheet of construction paper.
2. Place a sheet of waxed paper over the drawing.
3. Dip a piece of yarn in the glue and use it to outline the star design on the waxed paper. (Press the sheet of waxed paper down so you can see the design clearly.) While the glue is still wet, sprinkle the yarn with glitter.
4. Let the glue design dry overnight.
5. Peel the dried yarn star off and add a loop of yarn for hanging.

Make several stars to use as Christmas tree decorations, to hang in a window or as package tie-ons.

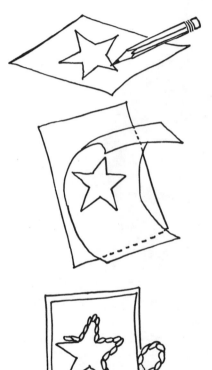

PAINT WITH PAPER

WHAT TO USE:
- various kinds of paper (newspaper, crepe paper, notebook paper, parchment)
- cardboard
- glue
- scissors

WHAT TO DO:
1. Begin to form a picture by arranging pieces of paper on the cardboard. You may want to tear some or burn the edges for interesting effects. (Be sure to ask for help when you do this.)
2. Make a landscape, city scene or a picture of something you like to do.
3. Glue the pieces on the cardboard. If you want, you can use a piece of plastic wrap to help preserve your picture.

WEAVE IT AND LEAVE IT

WHAT TO USE:
- three colors of construction paper
- scissors
- glue

WHAT TO DO:
1. Make slits in one piece of construction paper about one inch apart all the way across the sheet, leaving a one-inch solid border around the edges.

2. Cut strips of construction paper from the two other colors.
3. Weave one strip *over* and *under* the slits cut in the paper. Repeat with a strip of the second color, taking care to weave *under* and *over* this time.

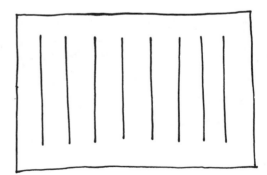

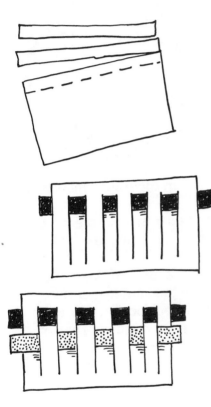

4. Continue weaving strips of the two colors in this manner until the entire paper is filled.
5. Glue the edges to prevent the strips from slipping out.

Use and enjoy your creation as a place mat, fold it to make a booklet cover or glue two or three together to make a table runner. After you have had some practice with weaving, you may want to try your hand at making woven hearts, baskets or boxes.

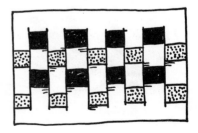

ALL BEADED UP

WHAT TO USE:
- any kind of white paper
- pencil
- glue
- paint
- scissors
- string

WHAT TO DO:
1. Cut thin strips of paper. Some can be rectangular, others you may want to vary the shapes.
2. Place a dab of glue on one side and roll the paper around the pencil.
3. When the glue dries, slip the beads off the pencil.
4. Paint the beads or sprinkle them with glitter and then string them into bracelets and necklaces. (You can also use colored construction paper for your beads.)

GLUE

20

FOILED AGAIN

Never, ever throw away a piece of foil.

Save big pieces such as the ones gifts are wrapped in, medium-sized pieces from cookie tins, stationery or candy boxes and even tiny bits from the inside flaps of envelopes.

Foil papers are especially nice because they are easy to cut and shape, and their nice shiny look adds a touch of "real class" to your "paper capers."

Foil can be used ...
- to cover boxes, bottles, cans and flowerpots
- for hats or costumes
- to make collages
- for three-dimensional paper sculptures
- to make holiday decorations

BIRDS OF A FEATHER
FLY TOGETHER

WHAT TO USE:
- construction paper (several colors)
- scissors
- glue

WHAT TO DO:
1. Cut a one-inch wide strip of paper.
2. Glue it together to make a loop about the size of your wrist. This will be the bird's body.
3. Cut another strip about one-half inch wide and about the size of a ring and glue it together. This will be the bird's head.
4. Glue the two circles together.
5. Cut a triangle-shaped piece and glue that on for the beak.
6. Cut wings from the paper and glue them on either side of the large circle.

To make a variety of different birds, you can add feet, lots of plumage or a crest.

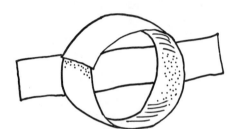

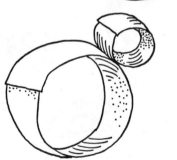

22

DOORKNOB DECORATIONS

You can use this very simple procedure to make doorknob covers or decorations to pep up every door in your house (or someone else's). Just remember to cut the round opening large enough to fit over the doorknob and to cut a few slashes around the circle to make it fit well.

Try some of these, then make up at least three of your own.

THE CHAIN GANG

WHAT TO USE:
- colored construction paper
- glue
- scissors

WHAT TO DO:
1. Cut strips from various colored construction paper.
2. Decorate or notch the strips if you want a "fancy" chain.
3. Glue the ends of one strip together to make a loop.
4. Add to your chain by threading a strip through the first loop and gluing the ends together.

You can drape these around the room for decorations or use them to make funny chain-link animals.

MARK THE PLACE WITH A SMILING FACE

Save every scrap of wallpaper or heavy gift-wrap paper (the embossed kind is especially good) to make bookmarks for yourself and to use as gifts. They make nice "tuck-ins" for cards or letters you plan to send or as package decorations.

All you do is cut a flower, tree or holiday symbol from a folded sheet of paper so that you have two identical shapes. Glue the two pieces together matching the front and back. Decorate with sequins or felt scraps. (You may want to add a ribbon or card to dangle, but it is not necessary.) Presto! You have a bookmark that shows your own special creativity.

MURAL, MURAL ON THE WALL

Mural making is one of the best ways to show off your "paper capers." Since you can use many different sizes and kinds of paper, it is a fine way to put valuable leftovers to good use.

Think about a theme or a story that you would like your mural to show. Then, take a sheet of drawing paper and sketch the picture you want to "paint." Use this sketch to design your mural.

Begin with a large piece of butcher paper or any other sturdy white paper. Plan your mural so that you can use both flat and three-dimensional figures to stand out from the background. Then, try to use as many of the other tricks you have picked up from this book to make an interesting mural — consider folding, rolling, curling, twisting, fringing and weaving to name a few.

27

BIRTHDAY BOOK BONANZA

Here's an easy way to make a birthday book to help keep track of the special people you want to remember on their birthdays.

WHAT TO USE:
- construction paper (12 different colors)
- glue
- felt tip pens
- hole punch
- scissors
- posterboard
- yarn

WHAT TO DO:
1. Use a different colored piece of construction paper for each month.
2. Fold up the paper from the bottom about three inches to make a pocket. Glue it together on either side.
3. Print each month on the pocket front, as well as the name, address and birthday of the person you want to remember. Do this for each month.
4. Punch two holes on the left side of each page.

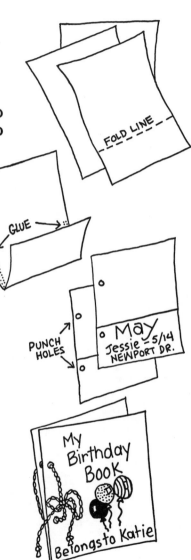

5. Make a cover for your birthday book from posterboard. Decorate it with felt tip pens and punch holes on the left side.
6. Tie the whole book together with pieces of yarn.
7. As you make special birthday cards for people you want to remember, put them in your book under the correct month. This way, you will have a month-by-month storage place for your handmade cards.

29

GREETINGS DESIGNED TO PLEASE

Almost everyone enjoys a visit to a card shop to browse and read the messages. Greeting cards come in all shapes and sizes, and if you look long enough, you can find one to suit almost any celebration. But, if you want to make someone extra happy on a special occasion, send them a greeting card designed especially for them and made by you. Once you begin making your own cards, you will find that your paper collection holds all kinds of goodies to add interest and special pizazz to your creations.

Begin with white paper that is stiff enough to fold, but thin enough to fit neatly in an envelope. Typing paper is just the right size to make a double-folded card. Simply fold the sheet of paper across the middle horizontally. Glue the paper together to form a nice sturdy card. Then, fold it vertically.

Now you are ready to create a design to make your card a "one-of-a-kind" surprise for the person who receives it. Begin by thinking about the person's special interest and use a theme related to a hobby.

Construction paper, bits of foil, paper doilies, gift-wrap ribbon or even felt or fabric can be cut and pasted to add to your design. You may want to cut out windows, doors, hearts, stars, etc. on the top fold of the card and draw or paste the design inside, or even use some of the paper tricks you have learned from this book.

31

My Star
xxoo

you're my

For a gardener, you might use a vegetable theme and actually work a package of seed into the design. For a person who enjoys needlework, a package of needles would be nice or a fisherman would surely enjoy a new fishing fly.

Here are a few ideas to get you started. Once you have had a little practice making your own cards, you will probably never want to send another store-bought card — that is unless you forget someone's birthday and it is too late to take the time to make a special card. To help you avoid this embarrassing situation, see the instructions for making your own birthday book.

Dear Grandpa,
HAPPY BIRTHDAY
I Hope you have a year filled full of good things!

A MANY-COLORED CREATURE AND HIS TWIN

WHAT TO USE:

- pencil
- two pieces of white paper
- several colors of crepe paper (the more the better)
- water
- sponge
- scissors
- glue
- black construction paper (for frame)
- large sheet of white paper
- felt tip pens

WHAT TO DO:

1. Lightly draw an outline of a fanciful creature on one piece of the white paper.
2. Tear or cut the crepe paper into small pieces to entirely cover the outline drawing.

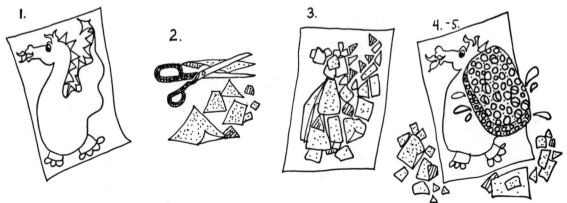

3. Arrange the crepe paper pieces inside the outline to completely cover the creature. Take the time to cut or tear the pieces as you work so that you have an interesting mosaic-type design.
4. Remove the crepe paper pieces, taking care to remember how you have the design worked out.
5. Dip the sponge in water and rub it over the white paper to thoroughly wet the surface.
6. Return the crepe paper pieces to their original positions to remake the design. (You will need to work quickly to get the pieces back in place before the paper dries.)
7. Place the second piece of white paper on top of the design and press it down hard with both hands.

8. Remove the top sheet of paper and discard the crepe paper pieces and you will discover not one, but two many-colored creatures looking at you. (The dye from the crepe paper will seep through both pieces of paper to make two outline shapes.)

9. Cut out the two creatures. Arrange them on one larger sheet of paper facing each other. Glue the creatures in place. Use a felt tip pen to draw in background scenery if you like.

10. Make a black construction paper frame and hang your many-colored creatures on the wall.

If you want, you can make small birds, flowers or holiday symbols to use on greeting cards. Your friends will wonder how you did it!

EASY ENVELOPES

To make an envelope to fit your own "designed-by-you" cards, draw it first on a sheet of white paper. Use a ruler to make the lines straight.

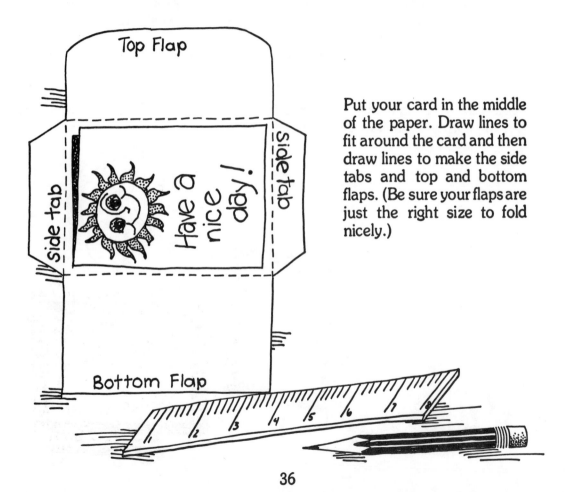

Put your card in the middle of the paper. Draw lines to fit around the card and then draw lines to make the side tabs and top and bottom flaps. (Be sure your flaps are just the right size to fold nicely.)

Cut and fold your envelope. Close, seal, add a stamp and your greeting is on the way. Once you get the hang of making envelopes, you will probably want to make some sturdy ones from construction paper or brown paper bags to hold puzzles, games or collections. Fancy envelopes made from wallpaper make great gift containers for stationery, photographs, recipe cards, etc.

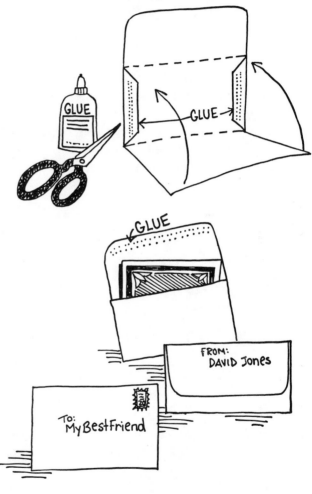

FUN AND FANCY HATS

Come To A Party

1. Cut a piece of construction paper as shown.
2. Form a cone and glue together.
3. Add designs with felt tip pens.
4. Punch small holes with scissors and add a string to keep it on your head.

A King Or Queen For A Day

1. Cut a long strip from construction paper like the one shown.
2. Glue the ends together and decorate with glitter.

38

There are lots of hats you can make if you just use a little imagination and some of the paper scraps you will find about the house.

You can turn even the dullest day into a new adventure by placing the "crowning" touch on your head!

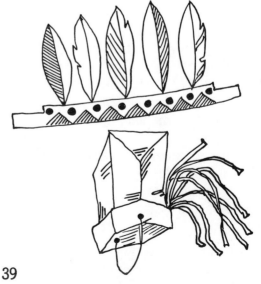

39

KALEIDOSCOPE DESIGNS

If you have ever looked through a kaleidoscope, you know that what you see is a view transformed into different images. The kaleidoscope helps you see things in a new and surprising way. Right before your eyes, the same colors, shapes and sizes form a new design.

Make some kaleidoscope designs of your own to decorate greeting cards, booklet covers or to back with felt and use for coasters.

WHAT TO USE:
- construction paper
- white or manila paper
- glue
- tissue paper (as many colors as possible)
- a small glass
- scissors
- pencil

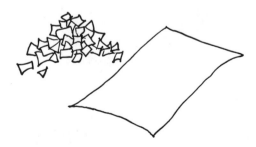

WHAT TO DO:

1. Tear the tissue paper into tiny little bits (almost like confetti).
2. Completely cover the surface of a sheet of construction paper with glue.
3. Hold a handful of the tissue paper pieces over the paper. Open your hand and let them fall. Spread the pieces out and pat them into the glue. Continue doing this until the whole sheet is covered with the tissue paper bits.

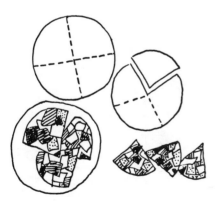

4. Trace around the bottom of the glass to make circles on the construction paper. Cut out the circles. Trace and cut out circles of the same size from the white or manila paper.
5. Divide the tissue-covered circles into four wedges (as you would cut a pie).
6. Place the wedges on a white or manila circle, using two or three to form kaleidoscope designs. Make as many as you have wedges for. You may be surprised at how different the designs can be from the same "paste-up."

FRAME-UPS

Use construction paper or tagboard to make frames for your artwork.

You will need two sheets of paper the same size and color and approximately one size larger than the drawing or painting that you want to frame.

1. Lay one sheet of paper flat on the table. Place the artwork on this sheet and trace around it. Cut out the inside section leaving just the frame.
2. Then, paste the artwork onto the other sheet of paper so that it will be centered inside the frame. Before pasting the "frame" in place, you may want to use a piece of clear plastic wrap to protect the artwork.

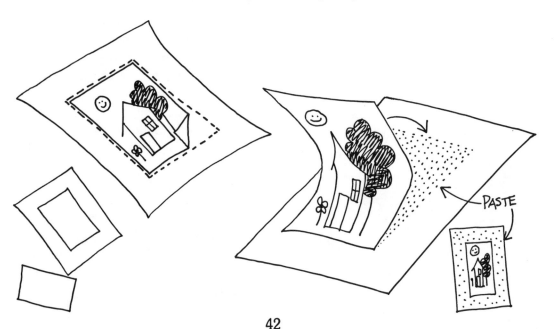

Cut out two large identical heart, flower or star shapes from construction paper. Cut out a "window" in one of the shapes. Glue a photograph of yourself onto the bottom shape so that it can show through the window. Then, glue on the shape with the "window."

Add a greeting, and you will have a very special card to send to someone who would appreciate a picture of you.

ON A ROLL

Before Columbus set sail, most people thought that the world was flat. That is the way some people look at paper. Without using your imagination, it is easy to look at paper as just a flat surface to write on, read from or wrap packages in. When you begin to experiment with the many ways you can make paper "stand up," you will see it in a whole new light. One of the easiest ways to do this is to make rolls. Cut your paper into strips the size and shape you want (short, narrow, wide, long). Then, roll the strips first in one direction then in another to see which way it rolls "naturally."

Experimenting with rolling paper into tubes is well worth the time it takes because these tubes can be used in so many ways. You can make chains, heads and bodies for puppets, sculptures, napkin rings, fun jewelry and many other things that will come to mind as you use the basic roll.

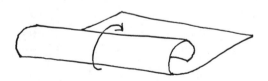

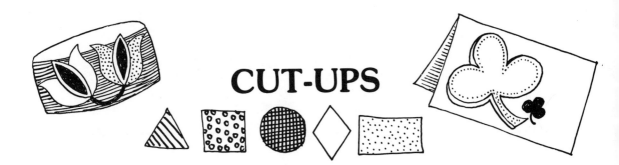

CUT-UPS

There are lots of things you can "shape up" by making all different kinds of decorative creations with shapes.

Cut out various shapes (triangle, square, circle, diamond, rectangle). Glue them on paper to make an interesting design. Then, use the "shape-ups" for borders, gift wrap or to cover an old wastebasket. Then, think up your own ways to use all the cut-ups you create.

TELL THE STORY

Want to surprise your teacher with a creative book report? Try one of these.

Fold a sheet of construction paper into four or five folds. Print the name of the book and the author on the first fold. Then, draw scenes to "tell the story" on each fold.

Make a mobile by stapling three strips of cardboard through the middle and adding a string for hanging. Cut circles from cardboard and draw scenes on each circle to "tell the story." Hang the circles from the cardboard strips to complete the mobile.

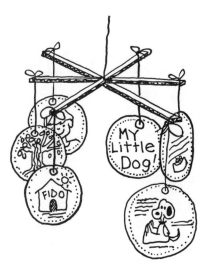

Make a poster from cardboard or construction paper to "advertise" the book.

Design and make a new cover for the book. "Tell the story" on the back of the cover.

MAGIC LANTERNS

WHAT TO USE:
- construction paper
- scissors
- tape or glue

WHAT TO DO:
1. Fold a piece of construction paper in half.
2. Along the folded side, carefully cut slashes, making sure they are evenly spaced. Leave approximately a 1½-inch border along each open side.
3. Open the paper and roll it into a tube lengthwise so the slashes run up and down.
4. Glue or tape the ends of the paper together.
5. Press the lantern in toward the center to help define its shape.

glue or tape

You can also make several of these in different colors to decorate for a party!

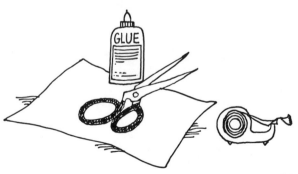

51

CIRCLE GO ROUND

WHAT TO USE:
- construction paper
- pencil
- string
- scissors
- saucer or small plate

WHAT TO DO:
1. Trace around a saucer or small plate to make a circle.

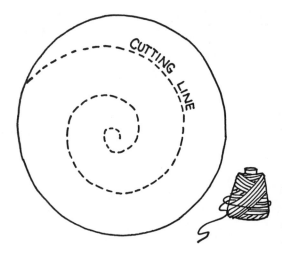

CUTTING LINE

2. Cut out the circle. Then, create a spiral by cutting into the circle at a slant, keeping the width even as you continue cutting.
3. Pull a string through the center of the spiral and knot it to form a hanger.

These make catchy and colorful party decorations, especially when two, three or four colors are used to carry out a specific theme.

THE TREE STANDS ALONE

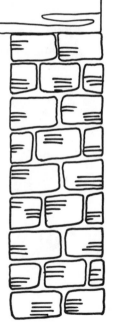

Cut two identical tree shapes from construction paper. Hold the pieces together and staple vertically through the middle. Then, fold the sides out to create a three-dimensional shape that will stand alone. By using different colors and sizes of paper, you can make a whole forest to decorate a window ledge or a mantel.

If you feel ambitious, you can cut out tiny birds, birds' nests, cones or berries to paste on the trees. Touches of glitter or sequins may also be used to add extra sparkle.

RING-A-ROUNDS

Ring-A-Rounds are easy to make and look as if they take much longer to construct than they actually do. They can be used for napkin rings, place cards, to decorate packages or just for fun. Ring-A-Rounds can be made from almost any paper you have on hand. You can even combine two or three kinds of paper to give real interest to the finished product. This is also a nice way to use bits of scraps or recycled paper. The stand-up strip can be made from any stiff paper (such as construction paper or tagboard) and the decorative design from papers you may have less of (such as foil, lace doilies or fancy gift wrap).

All you need is paper, scissors, glue, felt tip pens and trim such as buttons, sequins or ribbon.

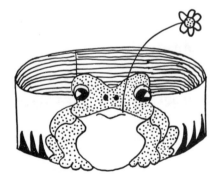

Here's what you do ...

1. Cut a strip of paper the size you want your Ring-A-Round to be.
2. Cut out a design and glue it to the center of the strip.
3. Glue the strip into a circle.

If you use your imagination, you will come up with all kinds of ideas for your Ring-A-Rounds. They can be made into bracelets, party decorations or to hold special rolled up letters. Larger Ring-A-Rounds would be suitable to pep up a flowerpot, coffee cup or as a crazy kind of headband.

GLUE

CARDBOARD IS NOT BORING

Cardboard is actually just heavy paper. One good way to build a good collection of cardboard to use for your projects is to recycle cardboard boxes — candy, sweater, coat, shoe and stationery boxes are especially good because of their size and manageability. Save some heavier corrugated boxes, too. Some of the flat boxes you may want to save and store just as they are. Others you will need to cut into sections and store flat.

Some ways to use cardboard include making ...
- puppet stages
- posters
- stand up dioramas
- booklet backs
- slides for the grass
- cards

Posters
All Sizes
50¢ – $2.00
SEE ME!

TISSUE PAPER FLOWERS

WHAT TO USE:
- two different colors of tissue paper
- bread tie or rubber band

WHAT TO DO:
1. Fold one piece of tissue paper like a fan. Then do the same thing with the other piece.
2. Put them together and hold them in the center with the bread tie or rubber band.
3. Pull apart the tissue paper and fluff it up like a flower.

PEEP AND TELL

WHAT TO USE:
- shoe box
- scissors
- glue
- tape

- scraps of all kinds of paper
- felt tip pens
- cardboard or tagboard
- construction paper

WHAT TO DO:
1. Plan a scene to show in your peephole box.
2. Cut out the figures (animals, people, plants, etc.) for your scene from construction paper or something similar.

3. Draw on facial features, clothes, blossoms, etc. with felt tip pens.
4. Cut a flat piece of cardboard to fit neatly in the bottom of the box. Use this piece to make a "stage" for the figures. This will let you make several different scenes to use in the same box. You can then lift one scene out and put another in and use your box over and over.
5. Make a folded tab to glue on the bottom of each figure. Glue each tab in place on your "stage."
6. Cover the sides of the box with tissue paper or decorate it with felt tip pens.
7. Cut a "peephole" in one end of the box.

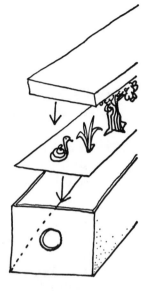

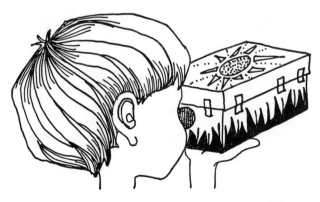

8. Put your completed scene in place and tape the top on the box.
9. Now you are ready for your friends to "peep and tell" you what they see.

TWO BY TWO

All the animals came in twos to Noah's Ark. If you can make just one, you'll have a head start!

Here are some of the materials you can use:
- all kinds of paper
- bathroom tissue and paper towel tubes
- paper cups and plates
- yarn, ribbon
- scraps of material
- string or twine
- felt tip pens
- other odds and ends

You will also need some scissors and glue.

Form lots of different animals using your wildest imagination and your best creative talents. Here are a few ideas to get you started.

BUG-A-BOO

Now, suppose Noah had wanted insects on board the ark rather than just animals. Make some from paper to get the procession started.

PAPER BUILDING PIECES

WHAT TO USE:
- paper
- scissors
- glue
- protractor or round object
- ruler
- pencil

WHAT TO DO:
1. Your paper can be most any kind — leftover wrapping paper, construction paper, etc. The first step is to cut out circles. Use a protractor or other round object to draw circles about three inches in diameter. Try folding the paper and cutting several circles at one time.
2. Trace a triangle in the circle and fold the circles into triangles.

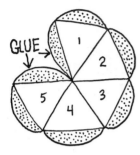

GLUE →

For a globe, you will need exactly 20 circles folded into triangles.

Glue five together along the folded edges to form a cone as shown at left. Glue five more in the same way.

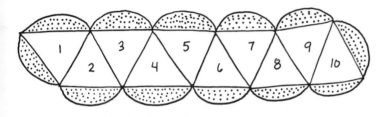

Glue ten circles together as shown here.

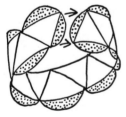

Then glue the ends together to form a ring.

Now glue a cone at each end of your ring to form a globe.

Add pipe cleaners and you'll have a satellite.

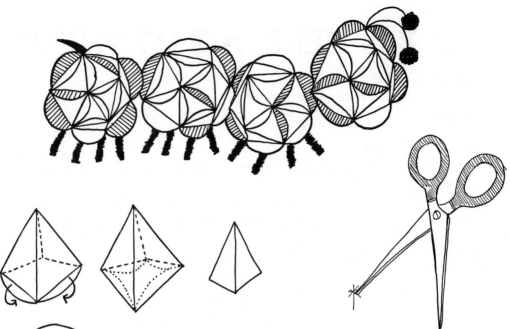

Glue several globes together to make a caterpillar.

Try folding circles into other shapes and glue them together to build all kinds of things.

A ZIG HERE, A ZAG THERE

WHAT TO USE:
- construction paper (two colors)
- glue

WHAT TO DO:
1. Cut two strips of paper the same length (one strip each of two different colors).

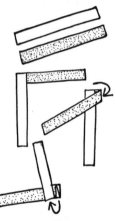

2. Put the end of one strip on top of the end of the other strip (at right angles) so that you have a square corner.
3. Glue the two strips together.
4. Fold one strip over the other, always keeping the folds at right angles.

5. Continue folding the strips one over the other until you reach the end. Then, paste the two end pieces together. You will now have an accordion-pleated fold which will spring back and forth and up and down.
6. Add cut out paper features to make a snake, puppet or jack-in-the-box.

ARMS AND LEGS —
COLLARS AND FRILLS

As you continue to follow the directions for making and enjoying the "paper capers" in this book, you will find lots of ways to use these zigzag paper folds.

They are great for puppet legs and arms, to add interest to holiday and seasonal mobiles and paper sculptures or to add extra flair to clowns, scarecrows, kings and queens.

SPRUCE UP SOME OLD STANDARDS

SAILING, SAILING

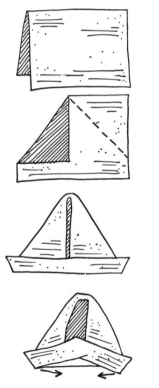

1. Fold a double sheet of newspaper in half along its center fold.
2. Fold the top corners into the center.
3. Fold up the bottom edges on both sides.
4. Open it up and put it on your head.

NOT-SO-NEWSY NOTES

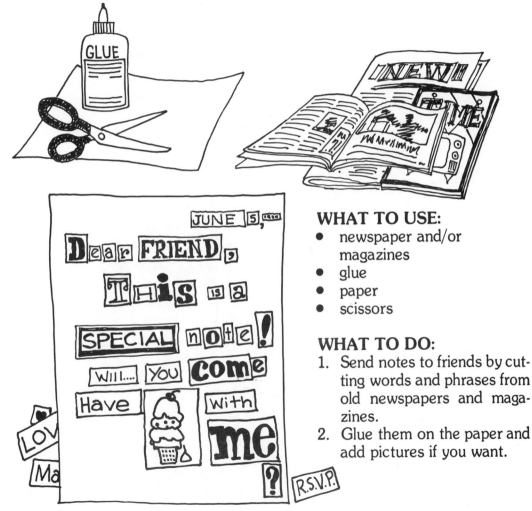

WHAT TO USE:
- newspaper and/or magazines
- glue
- paper
- scissors

WHAT TO DO:
1. Send notes to friends by cutting words and phrases from old newspapers and magazines.
2. Glue them on the paper and add pictures if you want.

WAYS TO USE PAPER BAGS

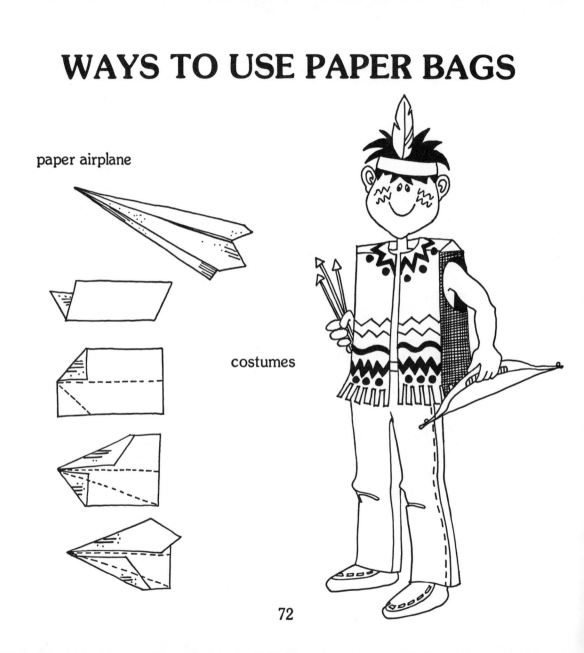

paper airplane

costumes

72

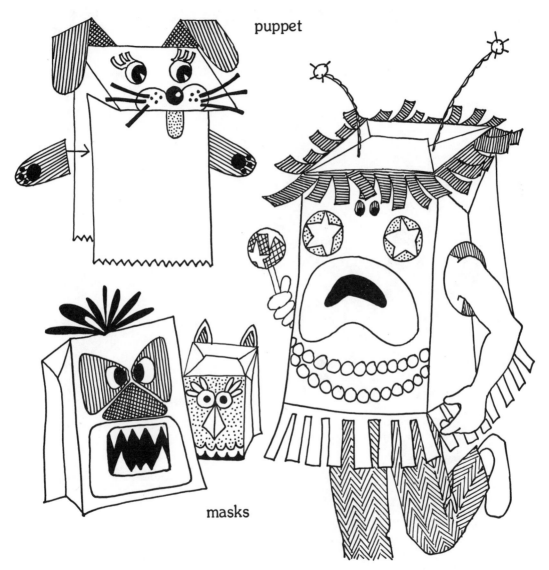

puppet

masks

73

WAYS TO USE PAPER PLATES

butterfly mobile

clock

mask

party hat

super holder

plate toss

75

WAYS TO USE PAPER CUPS

fancy planter

telephone

Christmas tree bells

Easter egg
basket

paper cup basketball

paper cup people

maracas

77

INDEX

A
airplane, 72
angel wings, 13
animals, 24, 60-61

B
basket, 76
basketball, 77
beads, 20
bells, 76
birds, 22
birthday book, 28-29
book covers, 18-19, 40-41, 49
book reports, 48-49
bookmarks, 25
borders, 47
bracelets, 20, 55
bugs, 62

C
cardboard, 56
cards, 30-32, 40-41, 43
caterpillar, 65
chains, 24
clock, 74
coasters, 40-41
collage, 17
costumes, 72
creatures, 33-34
crepe paper, 33-35
crown, 38

D
diorama, 58-59
doorknob covers, 23

E
Easter egg basket, 76
envelopes, 36-37

F
fans, 12-13
flowers, 57
foil, 21
folding, 13, 63-65, 66, 67
frames, 42-43

G
games, 75, 77
gift wrap, 47
greeting cards, 30-32, 40-41, 43

H
hats, 38-39, 70, 75
headband, 39
holder, 75
holiday decorations, 13, 16, 23, 25, 53, 54-55, 63-65, 76

I
insects, 62

K
kaleidoscope designs, 40-41

L
lantern, 50-51

M

maracas, 77
masks, 73, 74
mobiles, 49, 74
mosaic design, 33-35, 40-41
mural, 26-27

N

name
    cut-out, 14
napkin rings, 54-55
necklaces, 20
newspaper, 70, 71
notes, 71

P

package decorations, 16, 25
paper bags, 39, 72-73
paper building, 63-65
paper cups, 76-77
paper plates, 74-75
party decorations, 50-51, 52
party hats, 38, 75
place mats, 15, 18-19
planter, 76
poster, 49
puppets, 73

Q

quilt design place mats, 15

R

ring-a-rounds, 54-55
rolling, 46

S

sailor's hat, 70
satellite, 64
shapes, 47
shoe box, 58-59
spiral, 58-59
star, 16
stencils, 14
story telling, 26, 48-49

T

table runner, 18-19
telephone, 76
tissue paper, 40-41, 57
trees, 53

W

weaving, 18-19